NOW YOU CAN READ ABOUT....

SPACECRAFT

TEXT BY STEPHEN ATTMORE

ILLUSTRATED BY TONY GIBBONS

BRIMAX BOOKS • NEWMARKET • ENGLAND

We have lift-off! Up goes the rocket. Look for the spacecraft at the top. It is only a small part of the rocket. Huge tanks full of fuel are below it. This spacecraft is on its way to the Moon.

How does a space rocket move? It is like a firework rocket. Fuel is burned inside. This makes hot gases. Look for the stream of hot gases escaping from the rocket. The force of the gases pushes the rocket along.

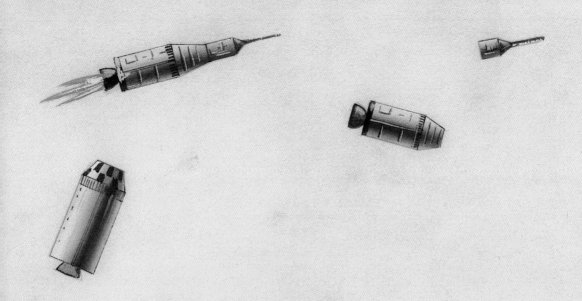

This space rocket has three
stages. As each stage runs out of
fuel, it falls away. The next stage
fires. Then the space rocket can
go faster. It goes higher and
higher. Look for the spacecraft
on its own. It is now in space.

Here is Robert Goddard standing
beside the rocket he built in
America. It flew for two seconds.
It reached a height of 13 yards.
Well, that was a record in 1926!

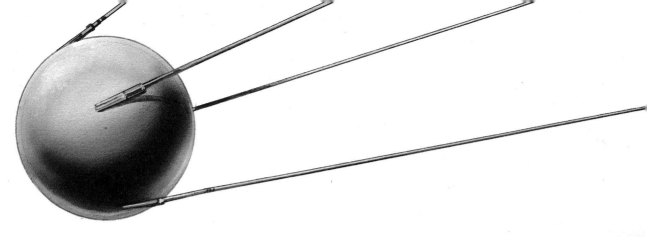

In 1957 the
Russians sent
this strange
thing into orbit.
As it circled the
Earth, it sent out
radio signals.
One year later
the Americans
sent a satellite
into space. Here
is the rocket
before lift-off.

This Russian spacecraft is called
Vostok 1. The artist has cut away
part of the spacecraft. Look for
the pilot. He was the first person
to go into space. The round
bottles were filled with air.
The pilot breathed this air.

The year is 1969. This American
spacecraft is in orbit round the
Moon. The landing craft is going
down on to the Moon. Two men are
inside it. They are the first
humans to visit the Moon.

This is a Russian space station.
Teams of Russians are taken up in
smaller spacecraft. They stay at
the space station for many days.
The long arms are solar panels.
They take heat from the Sun and
make it into electricity.

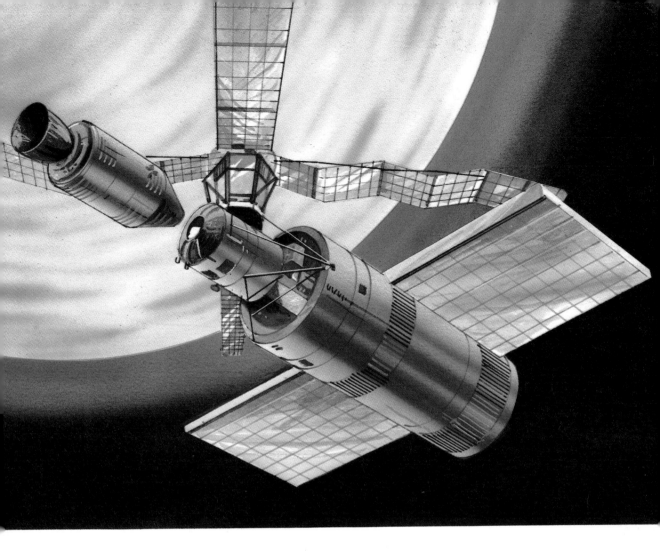

This American space station is
Skylab. The solar panels are like
the arms of a windmill. Look for
the spacecraft about to link up
with Skylab. The people inside
the small spacecraft are going to
work at the space station.

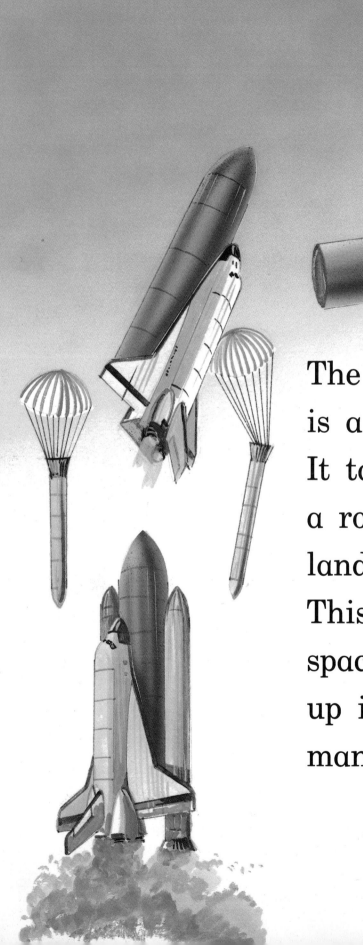

The space shuttle
is a space plane.
It takes off like
a rocket, but
lands on a runway.
This American
spacecraft can go
up into space
many times.

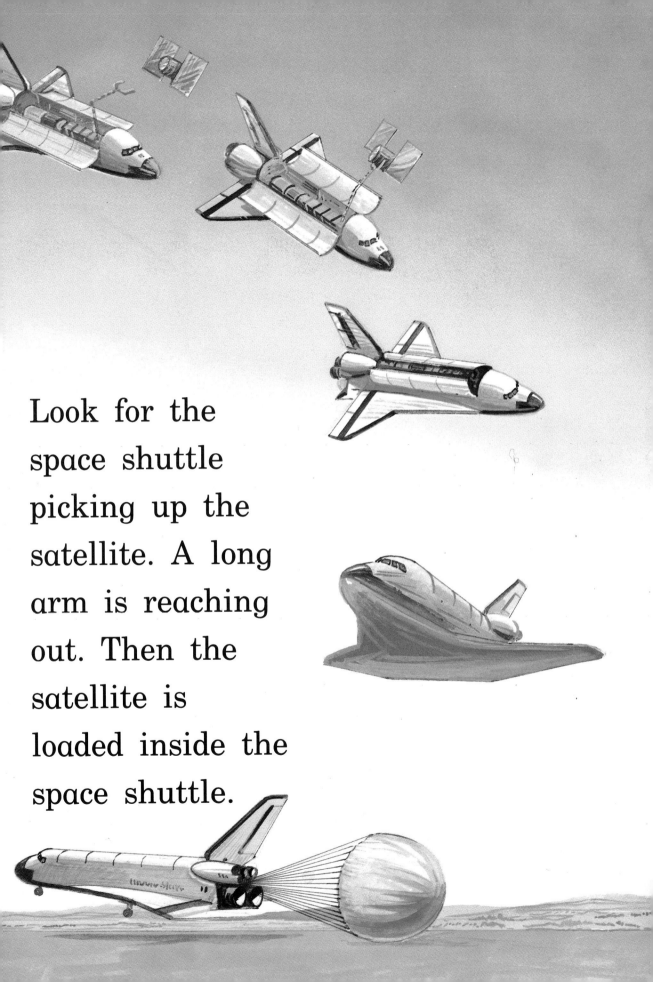

Look for the
space shuttle
picking up the
satellite. A long
arm is reaching
out. Then the
satellite is
loaded inside the
space shuttle.

Look at this space capsule
falling back to Earth from space.
It is re-entering the Earth's
atmosphere. The capsule is going
very fast. It is getting very hot.
It has a special heat shield.

The capsule has splashed down in the sea. Look at the outside of the capsule. The heat shield is damaged. It is peeling off. This happened when the capsule re-entered the Earth's atmosphere.

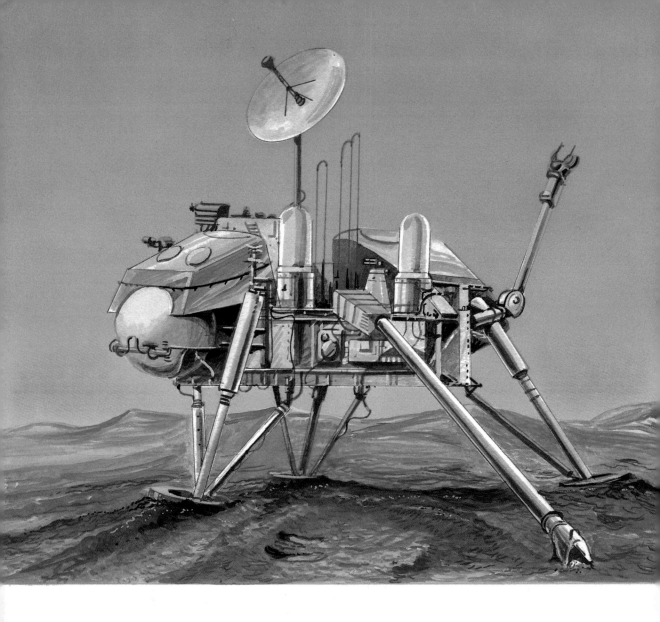

This American spacecraft is
a long way from Earth. It is on
the planet Mars. Look at the red
sands and pink sky. Some planets
are a long way away. Spacecraft
travel for years to get to them.

This Russian craft is going through the air above Venus.

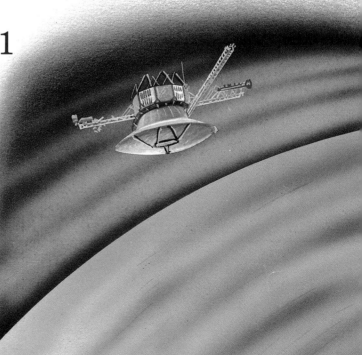

This American craft is flying past the planet Mercury. It looks like the Moon.

Here is Voyager 1 passing Saturn. The rings are made of millions of small rocks covered with ice.

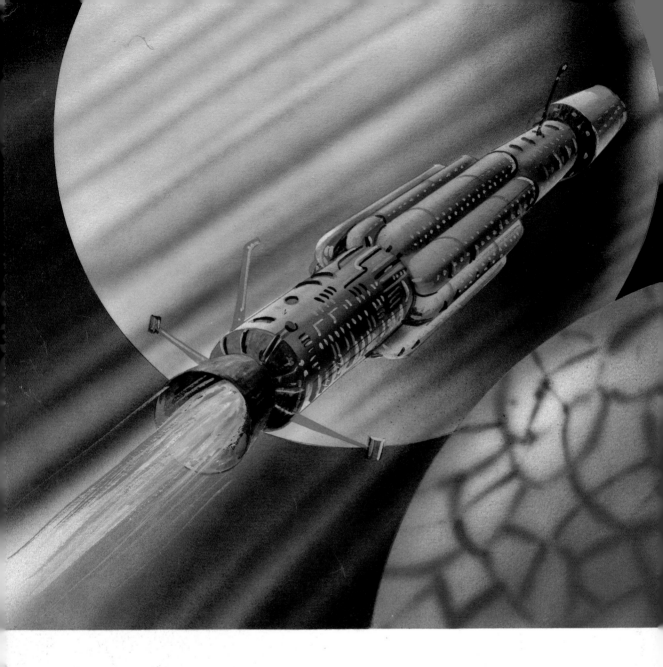

What will happen in the future?
Perhaps spacecraft will travel to
the stars. They are so far away
that we will need a very powerful
rocket. It might look like this.

One day people might live in giant spacecraft. Look at this monster craft. Would you like to live in space?

In this book you have read about spacecraft. Can you name these space vehicles? What are they doing?

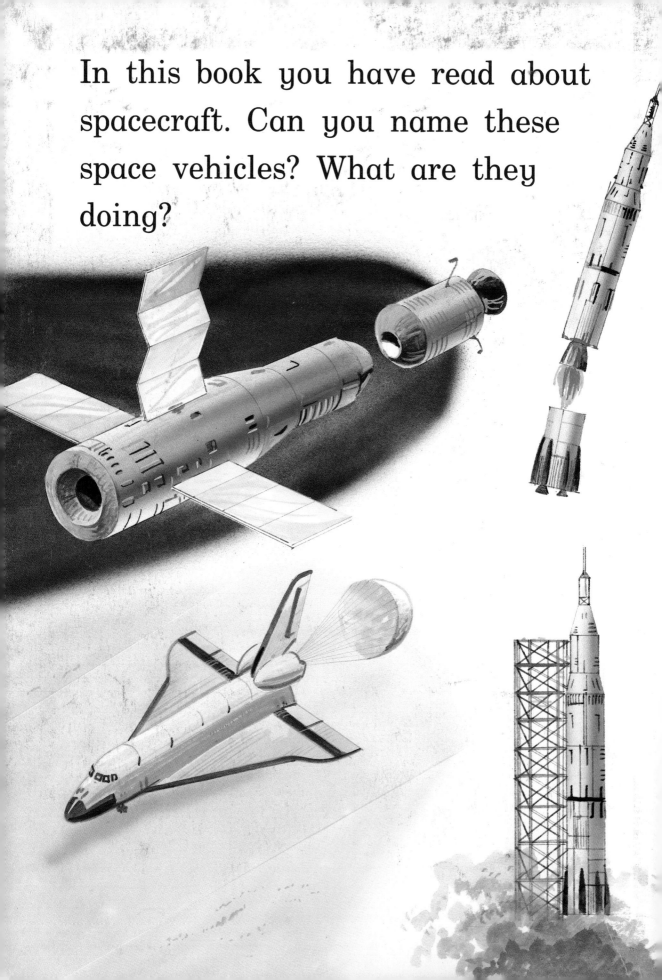